WORKING BY THEIR SIDE

A Guided Journal for Caretakers of
Loved Ones Facing an Eating Disorder

Lara Lyn Bell

Written by a collection of families, friends, and healed advocates.

BROWN BOOKS
PUBLISHING GROUP

Working by Their Side
A Guided Journal for Caretakers of Loved Ones Facing an Eating Disorder

Brown Books Publishing Group
16250 Knoll Trail Drive, Suite 205
Dallas, Texas 75248
www.BrownBooks.com
(972) 381-0009

A New Era in Publishing®

Publisher's Cataloging-In-Publication Data

Names: Bell, Lara Lyn, author. | Bell, Lara Lyn. By their side.
Title: Working by their side : a guided journal for caretakers of loved ones
    facing an eating disorder / Lara Lyn Bell ; written by a collection of
    families, friends, and healed advocates.
Description: Dallas, Texas : Brown Books Publishing Group, [2019] |
    Companion to book titled By Their Side.
Identifiers: ISBN 9781612543277
Subjects: LCSH: Eating disorders--Problems, exercises, etc. | Eating
    disorders--Patients--Care--Problems, exercises, etc. | Eating
    disorders--Patients--Family relationships--Problems, exercises,
    etc. | Caregivers--Problems, exercises, etc. | LCGFT: Problems and
    exercises.
Classification: LCC RC552.E18 B452 2019 | DDC 616.85/26--dc23

ISBN 978-1-61254-327-7
LCCN 2019938787

Printed in the United States
10 9 8 7 6 5 4 3 2 1

For more information or to contact the author,
please go to www.ByTheirSideBook.com.

Contents

This book is published with special thanks to all the wonderful people at Brown Books Publishing Group.

Before You Begin

Research shows putting our feelings into words produces therapeutic effects in the brain. Journaling takes the healing process to a deeper level, and we experience a greater benefit when writing down our thoughts.

In addition to reading By Their Side, working simultaneously in the companion book will be one of the caretaker's greatest assets in their journey—a personal anecdote improving their understanding of the caretaker role and their relationship with others and with their own self. It will put them steps ahead in the therapeutic process as they walk toward health and healing.

—Bethany Haley Williams, PhD, LCS
Founder and CEO of Exile International

Who Is This Book For?

This companion piece to *By Their Side* was conceived of as a study guide to help you, the reader, further your education by answering questions, dictating thoughts, recording uncertainties, and taking notes as you learn about your role as a caretaker to a loved one struggling with an eating disorder. The questions and prompts are taken directly from *By Their Side*.

Just like *By Their Side*, this book is intended to help you achieve a deeper understanding of the complexities of an eating disorder as well as a deeper awareness of yourself and your loved ones. This will help you decipher, identify, and manage your discomfort along your journey. Healing is hard work—we know!—but worth it. Work in this companion piece simultaneously as you read the book.

When you have completed this workbook, we highly recommend that you take your answers, research, and questions to an eating disorder professional who can help yourself and your loved ones. You will be many steps ahead in therapy and knowledge.

How to Use This Book

This companion piece is designed not only for freehand journaling but also as an orderly system for answering the questions posed throughout *By Their Side*. It follows *By Their Side* chapter by chapter, prompting the reader with reflective questions and enhancing their knowledge on every topic discussed in the book.

Why This Companion Piece Was Created

Research shows that writing and journaling relieve stress, help us think more clearly, and take worry from the brain to the page. In turn, this improves sleep, mood, and the performance of daily tasks.

> [Journaling is] an amalgamation of personal, rational fact-based reporting along with an exploration of your sometimes-irrational, always-important inner feelings. The thing about expressive writing and other types of journaling is that it's not just the act of processing your thoughts—something you could simply do by thinking about them—that brings about these massive benefits. It's the act of writing itself that seems to produce these results.[1]

We believe the companion piece will serve as a catalyst for understanding your role in healing.

Depending on where you are in your journey, you may wish to read *By Their Side* cover to cover while working along in the companion piece, or you may wish to work modularly. Take a moment to agree with yourself that you will be open and honest. Don't expect to have all the answers or to answer every question consecutively. There is no such thing as perfection. Just commit to doing the best you can in this moment!

We hope that by reading *By Their Side* and working in this companion piece, you will have an opportunity to redirect your own story.

---

1   Michael Grothaus, "Why Journaling Is Good for Your Health (And 8 Tips to Get Better)," Fast Company, January 29, 2015, https://www.fastcompany.com/3041487/8-tips-to-more-effective-journaling-for-health.

1 When You Suspect Your Loved One Has an Eating Disorder

In chapter 1 of *By Their Side*, we learn the types of eating disorders and associated behaviors that give us further clues into what is happening to our loved one. We learn how to identify, address, and take seriously the presence of an eating disorder in someone we care for.

As you respond to these questions below, spend some time reflecting on your loved one's recent behavior and what's been happening in their world—and in yours.

Do you believe there is a problem? If so, please explain.

_____

_____

_____

_____

_____

_____

_____

Denial is common in the first stages of eating disorders. None of us wants any of our loved ones to be sick. Are you possibly in denial about the serious nature of this illness? If so, why?

_____

_____

_____

_____

_____

_____

What have you observed about your loved one in recent months? Consider their behavior, appearance, relationships with friends, and behavior in school, at work, within their family, and with you. Please record your thoughts below.

_____

_____

_____

_____

_____

_____

_____

Has your loved one's behavior changed? In what ways?

_____

_____

_____

_____

_____

_____

Have you noticed changes in your loved one's behavior around food? Give an example of any changes or odd behavior you have witnessed around food and meals.

_____

_____

_____

_____

_____

_____

_____

When did you first start noticing a shift in your loved one's appearance or behavior?

_____

_____

• • • • • • • • • •

As you begin your journey, read the "Next Steps to Take Now" section of chapter 1, then take some time to research the following topics.

- The serious nature of eating disorders
- Behavioral characteristics of eating disorders
- The terms and definitions of eating disorders

Consider the sixteen characteristics mentioned in chapter 1, such as avoidance, sneakiness, withdrawal, tearfulness, increased anxiety, and being short tempered. Record your thoughts, feelings, and concerns about your loved one. Which, if any, of these sixteen characteristics do they currently exhibit? Do you see any of these characteristics in yourself?

_____

_____

_____

_____

_____

_____

As you learn more, you may be able to identify the eating disorder your loved one is struggling with, but do not try to diagnose your loved one. All eating disorders are complex issues that are often further complicated by coexisting conditions, so you will need to have your loved one assessed by an eating disorder specialist. However, your specific insights will be helpful to a professional making a proper diagnosis.

If you are not familiar with eating disorders, educate yourself on the categories defined in chapter 1 of *By Their Side*. Some of the more common types include:

- Anorexia nervosa (AN)
- Bulimia nervosa (BN)
- Binge-eating disorder (BED)
- Other Specified Feeding and Eating Disorders (OSFED)

For more information on other specified feeding and eating disorders (OSFED), including websites to consult in your research, see the appendix of *By Their Side.*

After reviewing the terms and definitions of eating disorders, do you feel knowledgeable about them? Make a list of questions you want answered by a professional.

_____

_____

_____

_____

_____

_____

_____

_____

_____

_____

In your mind, does your loved one manifest any of the symptoms described in your research on definitions of eating disorders? If so, please explain.

_____

_____

_____

_____

_____

_____

_____

_____

· · · · · · · · · ·

Do you identify with any of the realities we know to be true about eating disorders? What feels familiar? What new information did you learn?

_____

_____

_____

_____

_____

_____

As you observe these changes in your loved one, what do you notice about yourself?

_____

_____

_____

_____

_____

Are you able to communicate with your loved one? Is communication comfortable? Are conversations difficult? Give examples of what your communication currently looks like.

_____

_____

_____

_____

_____

_____

_____

_____

_____

• • • • • • • • • •

As you complete this chapter, reflect on what you've read, and record any additional thoughts or observations.

_____

_____

_____

_____

_____

_____

_____

_____

_____

_____

_____

_____

_____

_____

_____

_____

_____

_____

2 What Causes an Eating Disorder?

In chapter 2 of *By Their Side*, we consider causes and variables that can contribute to the development of eating disorders. We also learn that we can *never* be a perfect parent, friend, or caretaker. Being hard on oneself is not a solution; however, it is helpful to carefully reflect on how one's behaviors and actions may impact a loved one.

> Remember that eating disorders are complex conditions, often with many contributing factors. A single, definitive cause might be unidentifiable.

Do you think you know what caused your loved one's eating disorder?

_____

_____

_____

_____

_____

If unable to identify a possible cause of your loved one's disorder, can you instead commit to focusing on moving forward in helping your loved one heal? How will you do this?

_____

_____

_____

_____

_____

_____

Self-blame is counterproductive and can, in fact, be harmful to the healing process. Take a moment to write about any guilt you may be feeling.

_____

_____

_____

_____

_____

_____

Can you accept that you did not cause your loved one's eating disorder? If not, why?

_____

_____

_____

_____

Take some time to review the variables that can contribute to an eating disorder. Some possibilities include:

- Trauma
- Unhealthy family dynamics
- Bullying
- Depression

- Environmental risk factors
- Stress
- Codependency

> Sometimes the variables are clear; other times, we never identify the source of the behavior. Keep this in mind while you reflect.

Do any of the variables listed above or in chapter 2 feel familiar to you? Write about which variables you think might be contributing to your loved one's disorder.

_____

_____

_____

_____

_____

_____

While reading about genetics, temperament, predisposed brain chemistry, predisposed cognitive vulnerability, biological and physical sensation, and environmental risk factors, did you learn anything new? If so, journal about that discovery in the space below.

_____

_____

_____

_____

_____

_____

_____

_____

_____

_____

• • • • • • • • • •

Think about some of the common personality traits displayed by people suffering from eating disorders. Examples given in chapter 2 include:

- Perfectionism
- Overachievement
- People pleasing
- Attention seeking
- Obsessive-compulsive behaviors
- Anxiety
- Identity issues
- Low self-esteem
- Self-criticism
- Unhappiness with physical appearance
- Sensitivity
- Emotionality
- Peacemaking
- High intelligence
- Routine-oriented behavior
- Persistence
- Emotional Intelligence

Do you see any of these personality traits in your loved one? If so, describe the behaviors your loved one has been exhibiting. Do you recognize any of these traits in yourself or in other family members?

_____

_____

_____

_____

_____

_____

_____

_____

_____

While presenting challenges now, some of these personality traits can be positive with maturity. Which of your loved one's traits might prove positive? Take a moment to write about your loved one's potential.

_____

_____

_____

_____

_____

_____

• • • • • • • • • •

The intensity surrounding an eating disorder can draw parents, family members, and friends into codependent and enabling behaviors, which require thoughtful examination and adaptation to break. As you read the first four suggestions in the "Next Steps to Take Now" section of chapter 2, reflect on the following questions, and note your responses.

Do you find yourself blaming yourself or others? If so, why?

_____

_____

_____

_____

_____

_____

Guilt is common when dealing with eating disorders. Do you still feel guilty? If so, why?

_____

_____

_____

_____

_____

_____

_____

List ways you can forgive yourself, get beyond the guilt, and move forward for the sake of your loved ones and yourself.

_____

_____

_____

_____

_____

_____

_____

Are you riding your loved one's roller coaster—riding alongside their every emotion, causing you to fall prey to their temper, mood, or state of mind? If so, please explain what that looks like in your life.

_____

_____

_____

_____

_____

_____

Codependency is very common with eating disorders. Is your loved one codependent with you? If so, in what ways do you see yourself enabling them?

_____

_____

_____

_____

_____

_____

_____

Consider how you might begin setting boundaries. We recommend asking a professional to first help you identify codependent or enabling behaviors and then help you develop boundaries that are specific to your situation. *Boundaries*, a *New York Times* best seller by Henry Cloud and John Townsen, is an excellent resource, as is Pia Mellody's work on codependency and boundaries.

Journal about ways in which you feel you are an advocate for your loved one. Then list ways you may be hindering your relationship with your loved one.

_____   _____

_____   _____

_____   _____

_____   _____

_____   _____

_____   _____

_____   _____

_____   _____

_____   _____

_____   _____

What are some ways you can take better care of yourself so you can be strong and grounded for your loved one?

_____

_____

_____

_____

_____

_____

· · · · · · · · · ·

Parenting a child with an eating disorder can feel very lonely. You will need to build a village of support. *Ask for help!*

Who can you reach out to in order to build your support team? Write down the names of nonjudgmental, compassionate, honest individuals who are experienced in taking care of a loved one who has struggled with an eating disorder. Consider who will be proactive in helping you move forward.

_____   _____

_____   _____

_____   _____

_____   _____

> There may be people who would like to be supportive but who, for whatever reason, cannot help you. Do not let this discourage you! Cross them off your list of potential supporters, and move along—your village is out there.

Write down the names of professionals you have researched here. If you have not yet reached out for help, now is the time.

_____   _____

_____   _____

_____   _____

_____   _____

_____   _____

_____   _____

_____   _____

· · · · · · · · · ·

As you complete this chapter, reflect on what you've read, and record any additional thoughts or observations.

_____

_____

_____

3   Are Eating Disorders Genetic?

In chapter 3 of *By Their Side*, we take a closer look at factors that can set the stage for an eating disorder, including temperament, emotional intelligence, risk factors, biology, predisposition, and genetics.

While reading about the five factors that can set the stage for an eating disorder, did you learn anything new? If so, journal about that discovery in the space below.

_____

_____

_____

_____

_____

_____

_____

_____

_____

_____

_____

_____

We also look into ways we can put one foot in front of the other and model a healthy relationship with ourselves and with others.

Some of the characteristics common to people with eating disorders are:

- Anxiety
- Intensity
- Sensitivity

- Perfectionism
- People pleasing
- High intelligence (IQ)

- High emotions
- Tenderheartedness
- Social dependency
- Ambition/overachievement
- Routine-oriented behavior

- Persistence
- High emotional intelligence (EQ)
- Harm avoidance
- Impulsiveness

Do you see any of these characteristics in your loved one? Please give examples.

_____

_____

_____

_____

_____

_____

_____

_____

Do you see any in yourself? Please give examples.

_____

_____

_____

_____

_____

_____

_____

_____

Take a minute to review this chapter's discussion of emotional intelligence (EI). EI, also referred to as EQ, is not just about intelligence; it is more about being self-aware, being aware of others, and managing emotions.

Is your loved one emotionally intelligent? If so, please explain.

_____

_____

_____

_____

Can you identify any risk factors your loved one might have experienced or been exposed to, such as trauma, competitive sports, a cultural obsession with beauty, situational stressors, or relevant factors in their family history?

_____

_____

_____

_____

_____

_____

Is there an immediate family member who is struggling with or has struggled with an eating disorder? Have you ever struggled with an eating disorder?

_____

_____

_____

_____

_____

· · · · · · · · · ·

Take a look at this chapter's "Next Steps to Take Now." Use the following organizer to plan out ways in which you can help your loved one. Consider your strengths as well as the areas in which you find it more difficult to be helpful. (For example: Do you work preventatively? Do you enable? Do you shame?) When you are ready, review this list with a therapist or counselor who specializes in eating disorders.

What Am I Good At?	What's Hard for Me?

Plans to Help

Take a moment to consider these deeply personal, self-reflective questions, and record your thoughts.

- Do you portray body image positively?

  _____

  _____

- How do you portray body image in relation to gender? Do you portray a positive female body image? A positive male body image?

  _____

  _____

- What is the relationship between your body image and the culture you grew up in?

  _____

  _____

- What did your culture teach you about your body? What do you teach your children about that culture and that messaging?

  _____

  _____

- How do your children define you as a parent?

  _____

  _____

- How do your loved ones perceive your relationship?

  _____

  _____

- Are you overbearing, controlling, critical, fault finding, judgmental, or negative? If so, how can you adjust these parenting traits? If not, how can you continue the cadence of positivity during this difficult time?

  _____

  _____

- Are you trying to be the "perfect" parent, or do you accept your mistakes while also loving your child and admitting your human shortcomings?

  _____

  _____

- Are your expectations reasonable, both for your loved one and for yourself?

  _____

  _____

- When you discuss issues with your loved one, do you handle their perspectives firmly but thoughtfully? Are you truly listening to hear what they are saying?

  _____

  _____

- Are you asking your loved one to be a part of your plan, or are you trying to understand their own?

  _____

  _____

- Do you nurture your loved one's self-esteem? If so, how?

  _____

  _____

- Do you help your loved one see their strengths? Do you discuss those strengths in positive ways?

  _____

  _____

- How do you cultivate self-worth and self-respect in your loved one and in yourself?

  _____

  _____

- If you have had or do have your own eating disorder, are you working toward your own recovery?

  _____

  _____

- Are you choosing to rejoice in the positives of life or dwell in the negatives?

  _____

  _____

- What is your relationship with the way the media depicts bodies and appearance?

  _____

  _____

- Are you mindful of your words? Do you:
  » Call your loved one fat or pudgy?
  » Comment on other people's bodies?
  » Compare your loved one to others?

  _____

  _____

- Do you allow for vulnerability in others and within yourself?

  _____

  _____

- Do you shame your own body or looks, or those of others, even in jest?

  _____

  _____

After answering the questions above, consider having a family discussion or a one-on-one conversation with your loved one. Many caretakers, especially parents, struggle to communicate with their children. Please know that this is common. *Ask for help!* A qualified professional therapist can be invaluable in helping you navigate these sensitive conversations.

If you choose to engage your family in conversation, prepare yourself mentally and emotionally for these discussions ahead of time, as you don't want to overreact to honest responses.

• • • • • • • • • •

As you complete this chapter, reflect on what you've read, and record any additional thoughts or observations.

_____

_____

_____

_____

_____

_____

_____

_____

_____

_____

_____

_____

_____

_____

_____

_____

_____

_____

_____

_____

4   Getting Professional Help For Your Child

We cannot fix our loved one's eating disorder alone; we need to seek help. In chapter 4 of *By Their Side*, we discuss early intervention, finding help for your loved one, types of therapy and intervention, resources, and questions to consider when hiring a therapist.

As you review this chapter's "Next Steps to Take Now," reflect on the following questions, and note your responses.

Is your loved one in medical danger? If so, where can you take them for immediate help?

_____

_____

There are many different types of professionals who can help you and your loved one on your journey toward healing. Review the types listed in the book, and take notes in the space below. Some suggestions:

- Psychiatrists who specialize in eating disorders
- Licensed therapists who specialize in eating disorders, including:
  » Psychologists
  » PhDs
  » Counselors
  » Social workers
  » Faith-based therapists
  » Family therapists
- Physicians who specialize in eating disorders
- Dieticians and nutritionists

> *By Their Side* contains resources to help you understand therapy and find a suitable professional in the appendix and in the "Seek a Therapist for Your Child" section of chapter 4.

Have you had your loved one assessed by a professional? If not, whom can you call now to set up an appointment for diagnosis? Take notes here on any referrals.

_____

_____

_____

_____

_____

_____

_____

Do you understand the intentions of therapy? If not, what questions do you have? Consider discussing your questions with a therapist.

_____

_____

_____

_____

_____

_____

_____

Once diagnosed by a specialist, it's time to secure a therapist. Have you hired a therapist who specializes in eating disorders?

_____

_____

_____

_____

Take a moment to review chapter 4's list of questions we suggest you ask both before and after you hire a therapist. Write down the ones that are particularly relevant to your and your loved one's situation, then add your own specific ideas to the list.

_____

_____

_____

_____

_____

_____

_____

_____

_____

_____

_____

Make a list of potential therapists. Remember to take notes when you meet with them!

_____

_____

_____

_____

_____

_____

_____

_____

· · · · · · · · ·

Eating disorders are diseases of secrecy. Remember that your eyes and ears just might be the ones closest to the truth. What important information do you need to share with your loved one's therapist?

_____

_____

_____

_____

_____

_____

_____

_____

· · · · · · · · · ·

Use this space to keep track of referrals, people you have been in touch with, people you want to reach out to, potential mentors, and other resources you encounter as you seek healing for your loved one.

_____

_____

_____

_____

_____

_____

_____

_____

_____

_____

_____

_____

_____

_____

_____

_____

_____

_____

_____

_____

• • • • • • • • • •

As you complete this chapter, reflect on what you've read, and record any additional thoughts or observations.

_____

_____

_____

_____

_____

_____

_____

_____

_____

_____

_____

_____

_____

5 Finding Your Strength

In chapter 5, we reflect on the important role that we play when a loved one is facing an eating disorder. We learn the importance of intuition and the validity of listening to our gut.

Sometimes going with your gut can be difficult. For example, your gut might be telling you that your loved one needs to go to treatment, but many factors could make this a hard decision, and you might find yourself fighting against the facts. Perhaps you know something is terribly out of balance but are having trouble facing the situation and really don't know what to do.

In the space below, journal what your gut has been telling you.

_____

_____

_____

_____

_____

_____

_____

_____

_____

_____

_____

_____

_____

• • • • • • • • • •

Who are the people on your support team? Make a list here as you continue to build your village of support.

_____   _____

_____   _____

_____   _____

_____   _____

_____   _____

_____   _____

• • • • • • • • • •

Review this chapter's "Next Steps to Take Now." Reflect, and note your responses to the following.

Do you practice a faith? If so, are you nurturing your faith?

_____

_____

_____

_____

_____

Do you exercise? Is your exercise routine balanced? Do you overexercise or compulsively speak about it? Has your loved one ever expressed anything about your exercise routine?

_____

_____

_____

_____

_____

_____

Is yoga an option for you? Make a list of the yoga studios convenient to your home or office, and try a class for beginners!

_____   _____

_____   _____

_____   _____

_____   _____

> Consider using a guided meditation app to begin your day with meaning and self-care! Calm (Calm.com) and Sam Harris's Waking Up (WakingUp.com) are two excellent places to start, but you should do your own research to find the guided meditation routine most applicable to your customs and lifestyle.

Close your eyes, and take one minute to visualize your loved one healthy. What does that look like?

_____

_____

_____

_____

_____

_____

_____

What music can you play in your home that will lighten the mood and soothe your family? What music makes you smile?

_____

_____

_____

_____

_____

Do you have a passion or hobbies? What are they? How can you make time for these in your current situation?

_____

_____

_____

_____

_____

_____

How can you better practice simple kindness in everyday life?

_____

_____

_____

_____

_____

Remember how important it is to ask for and receive help throughout your journey! You are not alone!

• • • • • • • • • •

As you complete this chapter, reflect on what you've read, and record any additional thoughts or observations.

_____

_____

_____

_____

_____

_____

6   Overwhelmed? Simplify!

In chapter 6 of *By Their Side*, we begin to look at ways that we can make life less hectic, such as learning coping skills, prioritizing family time, and balancing work and life. Living with a loved one who's facing an eating disorder can be extremely challenging, and the normal busyness and complexities of life can exacerbate the stress considerably.

As you look at your home and lifestyle, you might be at a loss as to how to begin simplifying to better promote a healing lifestyle. Here are some things to consider as you begin.

- Take a look at your place of residence, and ask yourself, "What makes our house feel like a home?"
- What comforts the people who live in your home, and what makes them want to spend time there?
- What can we let go of or change to make things function more smoothly during this difficult time?
- What music do we enjoy? Will playing it lift the mood of the home?

What simple changes to your home and daily routine might help to create a warmer, safer, and more welcoming atmosphere?

_____

_____

_____

_____

_____

_____

_____

_____

_____

Think about asking your family for their thoughts and opinions on this matter. Use this space to write down what, if anything, you discuss.

_____

_____

_____

_____

_____

_____

_____

_____

_____

_____

_____

_____

_____

_____

_____

In an effort to take better care of yourself and your family, fine tune your current needs. Once you understand what you want and need, it is easier to ask for those things and to implement them in your daily life, helping you feel replenished and restored. Remember, your state of mind, body language, and mood affect everyone around you.

Consider the following questions, and record your thoughts.

- What do you like?
- What do you need?
- What soothes you when you are stressed?
- What brings you peace and comfort?

_____

_____

_____

_____

_____

_____

_____

_____

How can you incorporate some self-care elements into your daily routine?

_____

_____

_____

_____

_____

What's the most challenging part of your day, and what are some little things that might help it be less challenging?

_____

_____

_____

_____

_____

_____

What do you most need help with right now? Who can you ask for help? Do you know anyone who has been down this road ahead of you?

_____

_____

_____

_____

_____

_____

What are your values, and what is most valuable to you?

_____

_____

_____

_____

_____

_____

· · · · · · · · · ·

Sharing quality time together, communicating honestly, respecting one another, learning new coping skills, managing time, and prioritizing family are consequential both to self-care and to building healthy relationships in the home. This chapter contains many suggestions about how to accomplish these goals. Please journal in the space below about the suggestions that are most relevant to your and your family's current situation.

_____

_____

_____

_____

_____

_____

_____

_____

_____

_____

_____

_____

_____

_____

Should you seek help for yourself from a professional? If so, why?

_____

_____

_____

_____

_____

_____

Respect is a two-way street. Have you established a relationship of respect? If so, how? If not, what can you do to improve the relationship?

_____

_____

_____

_____

_____

_____

If you are engaged in a relationship, are you sharing private time with your partner? Are date nights possible?

_____

_____

_____

_____

_____

_____

Is your family taking time to communicate? How is it going? What light topics—unrelated to the eating disorder your loved one is struggling with—can you bring up with your family?

_____
_____
_____
_____
_____
_____
_____
_____

Are you spending time together as a family? What activities can you do together?

_____
_____
_____
_____
_____

Would family therapy help to enhance communication within your family? If so, why do you feel this way?

_____
_____
_____
_____
_____
_____
_____
_____

If you have any other children in the house, have you appropriately educated them about your loved one's battle with their eating disorder? How can you help them to feel safe in such a scary and tumultuous time?

_____

_____

_____

_____

_____

_____

_____

_____

What nonessential activities can you let go of, both at work and socially?

_____   _____

_____   _____

_____   _____

_____   _____

_____   _____

_____   _____

What can you do to implement consistent mealtimes in your household? How can you make meals together meaningful, fun, and pleasant?

_____

_____

_____

_____

_____

_____

• • • • • • • • •

Remember, there is no such thing as perfection. How have you learned from the mistakes that you've made? What will you do differently next time?

_____

_____

_____

_____

_____

_____

_____

_____

_____

_____

_____

What does family time look like for you?

_____

_____

_____

_____

_____

_____

_____

_____

_____

_____

· · · · · · · · · ·

What responsibilities can you share with your spouse or partner? What responsibilities can the children and young adults living in your home help with?

_____

_____

_____

_____

_____

_____

What do you need to help you balance work and life?

_____

_____

_____

_____

_____

_____

What do you need at work? Whom do you need to speak with regarding your current situation? Is there a colleague who could help alleviate unnecessary stress? What projects can you shelve and get back to at a later time?

_____

_____

_____

_____

_____

_____

_____

Use the following organizer to make a to-do list. Consider urgent, short-term, and long-term tasks.

Urgent	Short-Term	Long-Term

• • • • • • • • • •

As you complete this chapter, reflect on what you've read, and record any additional thoughts or observations.

_____

_____

_____

_____

_____

_____

_____

_____

_____

_____

_____

7

Self-Reflection

As we learn in chapter 7, self-reflection means discovering more about who we are. While self-reflection isn't always easy, it can be eye opening and help us arrive at a more solid and grounded place within ourselves. Having a strong sense of oneself is critical when helping a loved one in recovery.

Review this chapter's "Next Steps to Take Now," and respond to the self-reflective questions below.

Are you grateful for your body? Give examples of why or why not.

_____

_____

_____

_____

_____

_____

Do you think you continue to add to your child's eating disorder? If so, how?

_____

_____

_____

_____

_____

_____

_____

Do you think your spouse, partner, or family unit compounded the eating disorder? If so, how?

_____

_____

_____

_____

_____

_____

Boundaries should not be a parental power play; instead, they should be affirmative and safe, set in such a way that your loved one will eventually recognize your good intentions. How can you be a benefit to your loved one's healing rather than a hindrance? Are you setting boundaries that will keep them safe? Give examples.

_____

_____

_____

_____

_____

_____

_____

_____

Your voice is powerful—both positively and negatively. Do you speak with firm but loving words that are mature and reflective? Give examples.

_____

_____

_____

_____

Do you listen without judgment? If so, how? If not, what can you do to improve your listening skills?

_____

_____

_____

_____

_____

_____

Body language communicates so much. A slight frown or an unhappy expression can immediately give a loved one an impression of anger or disengagement, even if those aren't the feelings you're trying to convey. Do you pay attention to your own body language? Give examples.

_____

_____

_____

_____

_____

_____

Do you lose your temper easily? Often, a loved one's anger, grief, frustration, or pain can trigger our own. When this happens, we are no longer present to allow our loved ones space to express their important emotions. Find help with your own emotions so you can make space for those of your loved one. What might you do to prevent outbursts?

_____

_____

_____

_____

_____

_____

Do you celebrate a B or demand an A+? (See chapter 7 of *By Their Side*.)

_____

_____

_____

_____

_____

_____

Are you using your loved one's success to make up for your own lack of feeling successful or having a purpose? Can you give examples?

_____

_____

_____

_____

_____

_____

Have you asked for support from family and loved ones? Who have you asked? Who should you ask?

_____   _____

_____   _____

_____   _____

_____   _____

_____   _____

_____   _____

_____   _____

_____   _____

Have you made efforts to build a village of support?

Do you love yourself? In what ways do you demonstrate that?

_____

_____

_____

_____

_____

Can you love unconditionally? What does that look like for you?

_____

_____

_____

_____

_____

_____

Would you benefit from therapy? How so?

_____

_____

_____

_____

_____

_____

_____

Are you fighting the battle alone? For whom or for what are you fighting?

_____

_____

_____

_____

_____

What self-care practices work for you? List them here.

_____   _____

_____   _____

_____   _____

_____   _____

_____   _____

Are you taking time out of the day for yourself? What does that look like, and how does doing so benefit your spirit, mind, and soul? How is it impacting those around you in positive ways?

_____

_____

_____

_____

_____

_____

_____

Are you writing openly and honestly in this companion piece?

· · · · · · · · · ·

As you complete this chapter, reflect on what you've read, and record any additional thoughts or observations.

_____

_____

_____

_____

_____

_____

_____

_____

_____

_____

_____

_____

_____

_____

_____

_____

_____

_____

_____

_____

_____

_____

_____

8 Strengthening Your and Your Family's Emotional Health

In chapter 8, we learn the importance of strengthening our own emotional health and that of our family. Take a minute to write a list of emotions that you are feeling right now. What could be healthy outlets through which to express these emotions? Do you need help working through any of them?

_____

_____

_____

_____

_____

_____

_____

_____

_____

_____

_____

_____

_____

_____

_____

_____

_____

_____

· · · · · · · · · ·

Review this chapter's "Next Steps to Take Now," and respond to the questions below.

Break and reset. Are you allowing yourself to cry? Are you afraid of being vulnerable? If so, why?

_____

_____

_____

_____

_____

_____

_____

Forgive and learn. Can you forgive yourself for mistakes that you have made? Can you forgive your loved one who is sick? How will you do this?

_____

_____

_____

_____

_____

_____

_____

Nurture your family. How will you deal with your loved one's intense emotional state while nurturing your relationships with other family members? Who can you call to help you find a family therapist if you don't already have one?

_____

_____

_____

_____

_____

_____

_____

_____

Communicate honestly and openly with your spouse, partner, or significant other. Do you need marriage or couples counseling? What do you need from your spouse during this time of unrest? What does your spouse need from you, and are you able to meet those needs?

_____

_____

_____

_____

_____

_____

_____

_____

Use this space to reflect on your behavior with others—for instance, with your spouse or loved one. Make notes on ways you might wish to step back and change how you've engaged with them.

_____

_____

_____

_____

_____

_____

_____

_____

_____

_____

_____

_____

_____

_____

_____

_____

Make a list of challenges and obstacles you want to discuss with a trusted friend, counselor, clergy, therapist, or support person. In the lines below, describe some of the emotions you are having right now. It is OK to be angry, resentful, or hurt. If you are feeling this way, please make that call for help!

_____   _____

_____   _____

_____   _____

_____   _____

_____   _____

_____

_____

_____

_____

_____

_____

_____

· · · · · · · · ·

As you complete this chapter, reflect on what you've read, and record any additional thoughts or observations.

_____

_____

_____

_____

_____

_____

_____

_____

_____

_____

_____

_____

_____

_____

_____

_____

_____

_____

_____

_____

_____

_____

_____

_____

_____

_____

_____

9   Get Professional Help for Yourself

As you are learning, caregivers need lots of care themselves. If you haven't already, please consciously begin building your personal support team—people who are available for and supportive of you. The focus right now might be on your loved one and their eating disorder, but you, too, need to avail yourself of your own support team.

Make sure you understand your own innate temperament. Take one of the personality tests referenced in this chapter of *By Their Side* to help you learn to communicate better. Of the four tests described, we first recommend that each family member take the Enneagram. It's actually quite fun, and there is absolutely no judgment on the outcome of the test. You might be surprised by how differently you and your family members respond in different situations. For suggestions on more personality tests, see the appendix.

You can find a detailed description of the Enneagram at Integrative9.com. The official test requires a fee, but free testing can be found on several online sites, including:

- LonerWolf.com/enneagram-test/
- EclecticEnergies.com/enneagram/test
- GrowthMarketingPro.com/enneagram-personality-test/

Another fun and easy personality to test to do with your family comes from Gary Chapman's *The Five Love Languages*. The quiz at 5LoveLanguages.com can help you better understand your love language and improve your communication skills. It is a nonjudgmental way to better understand yourself and others. Chapman's book itself is also a very worthwhile read.

What is your love language? Explain below.

_____

_____

_____

_____

_____

• • • • • • • • •

If you are not already in therapy or counseling, perhaps it is time to secure a professional who has knowledge of and experience with eating disorders. Make a list of referrals to therapists. See the appendix of *By Their Side* for information about resources such as the National Eating Disorders Association (NEDA), the International Association of Eating Disorder Professionals (IAEDP), and EDReferral.

_____   _____

_____   _____

_____   _____

_____   _____

_____   _____

_____   _____

_____   _____

• • • • • • • • •

Review this chapter's "Next Steps to Take Now." Get referrals to counselors and therapists who are trained in working with eating disorders. Use this space to take notes during the consultation with a potential therapist. Make sure to obtain answers to the fifteen questions in chapter 9, whether face to face or over the phone.

_____

_____

_____

_____

_____

_____

_____

_____

_____

_____

_____

_____

_____

_____

_____

_____

_____

_____

_____

_____

_____

_____

_____

_____

_____

_____

_____

Use this space to list other questions you may have.

_____

_____

_____

_____

_____

_____

_____

_____

_____

_____

_____

_____

_____

Are you in couples therapy? Do you need to be? Why or why not?

_____

_____

_____

_____

_____

_____

_____

_____

Are you in family therapy? Do you need to be? Why or why not?

_____

_____

_____

_____

_____

_____

_____

If applicable, have you looked online to access more affordable information? (You will also discover other ways and means of affording treatment in chapter 13 of *By Their Side*.) Please take notes in the space below.

_____

_____

_____

_____

_____

_____

_____

_____

_____

_____

_____

_____

_____

_____

_____

_____

_____

_____

_____

_____

_____

_____

Who comprises your support team? We are going to continue to ask this question because no one should go through this alone! You do not have to!

_____   _____

_____   _____

_____   _____

_____   _____

_____   _____

_____   _____

_____   _____

· · · · · · · · · ·

As you complete this chapter, reflect on what you've read, and record any additional thoughts or observations.

_____

_____

_____

_____

_____

_____

_____

_____

_____

_____

_____

_____

10   Treatment and Various Options

In chapter 10, we strongly encourage you to take inventory of the options available to you and your loved one. We discuss a variety of treatment options, explore the importance of staying within your financial means, and suggest referrals that you can research.

Have you had your loved one diagnosed by a professional? If so, by whom? If not, why?

_____

_____

_____

_____

_____

_____

_____

_____

In *By Their Side*, we have listed five treatment options, but there are many more. If you are not familiar with the options available, please refer to the appendix for chapter 10. List any websites that you decide to research in the space below.

_____ _____

_____ _____

_____ _____

_____ _____

_____ _____

_____   _____
_____   _____
_____   _____
_____   _____
_____   _____

Follow this chapter's "Next Steps to Take Now." Most of the topics are educational, so please take notes. Use this space to make a list of mentioned
resources.

_____   _____
_____   _____
_____   _____
_____   _____
_____   _____
_____   _____
_____   _____
_____   _____
_____   _____
_____   _____

Are you educated on treatment options, such as inpatient, residential, IOP,
outpatient, and aftercare? If not, please take notes in the space below as
you begin reading about types of treatment.

_____
_____
_____
_____
_____
_____

_____

_____

_____

_____

_____

_____

Have you asked for help in seeking treatment options? Who can you ask? If you are working with professionals in the eating-disorder field, have you asked them for help?

_____   _____

_____   _____

_____   _____

_____   _____

_____   _____

_____   _____

By Their Side lists seven websites to research as you seek to find the most affordable and suitable treatment options for your loved one. Please take notes when you visit EDReferral, Eating Disorder Treatment Reviews, NEDA, ANAD, Eating Disorder Hope, the Treatment Specialist, and MEDA.

_____

_____

_____

_____

_____

_____

_____

_____

_____

_____

_____

_____

_____

_____

_____

_____

_____

_____

_____

Treatment is expensive. How are you going to stay within your means while offering your loved one the most suitable treatment possible? (Refer to chapter 13 of _By Their Side_ for further suggestions.)

_____

_____

_____

_____

_____

_____

List ways in which you are taking care of your physical and mental health.

_____

_____

_____

_____

_____

Do you feel gratitude to your body? How do you feel about your self-worth?
Do your loved ones know how you feel?

_____

_____

_____

_____

_____

_____

• • • • • • • • • •

As you complete this chapter, reflect on what you've read, and record any
additional thoughts or observations.

_____

_____

_____

_____

_____

_____

_____

_____

_____

_____

11 Registered Dietitians and Nutritionists

Chapter 11 of *By Their Side* is about dieticians and nutritionists. The information in this chapter, such as the importance of accreditation and the differences between dieticians and nutritionist, is primarily educational. We also highlight some controversial methods to avoid, suggest sites to research, and offer referrals.

After the introduction, you can begin reviewing this chapter's "Next Steps to Take Now." Please take notes in the sections below.

Do you feel like you are educated on the differences between types of accreditation? Can you distinguish between nutritionists and dieticians who are trained in eating disorders? If not, please reread the section entitled "Understand the Options and Differences between Dieticians and Nutritionists," and take notes below.

_____

_____

_____

_____

_____

_____

_____

_____

Are you actively looking for a suitable nutritionist or dietician for your child? Make a list of friends or acquaintances who have personal experience with specific dieticians or nutritionists who specialize in treating eating disorders. Call them, and ask for a referral.

_____   _____

_____   _____

_____   _____

_____   _____

_____   _____

_____   _____

If you cannot find a referral, contact the International Federation of Eating Disorder Dieticians, and enter your zip code to find help near you. Also search EDReferral.com or Eating Disorder Hope. More information on these resources can be found in *By Their Side*. Use the space below to take notes on your findings.

_____

_____

_____

_____

_____

_____

_____

_____

_____

_____

_____

_____

_____

_____

_____

Use this space to take notes during a preliminary consultation with a potential dietician or nutritionist. Gather relevant information using the list of questions in chapter 11 of *By Their Side* as a guide. It is wise to get this information before you commit to working with a particular professional to ensure that you are making the best decision for yourself and your loved one. (If you are seeking treatment with your spouse or partner, adjust the questions to reflect both of you as needed.)

_____

_____

_____

_____

_____

_____

_____

_____

_____

_____

_____

_____

_____

_____

_____

_____

_____

_____

_____

_____

_____

_____

"Intuitive social eating" is a term that we formulated for this book. It does not demand perfection with or around food. The goal of intuitive social eating is to recognize hunger signals, eat comfortably in social settings, and ease back into the normalcy of social bonding that occurs around shared meals. Remember, eating disorders are about underlying emotional issues. What are you witnessing now in your loved one's relationship with intuitive social eating?

_____

_____

_____

_____

_____

_____

_____

_____

_____

_____

_____

_____

If you need financial assistance, follow the suggestions in this chapter of *By Their Side*, and take notes. Consult with a NEDA Navigator, check out virtual IFEDD member dieticians, or go to the International Federation of Eating Disorder Dietitians website. You can also refer to chapter 13 for more information.

_____

_____

_____

_____

_____

_____

_____

_____

_____

_____

_____

_____

_____

_____

_____

_____

_____

_____

_____

_____

_____

_____

· · · · · · · · · ·

List any contacts, referrals, and websites here for your convenience.

_____   _____

_____   _____

_____   _____

_____   _____

_____   _____

_____   _____

_____   _____

_____   _____
_____   _____
_____   _____
_____   _____
_____   _____
_____   _____
_____   _____
_____   _____

• • • • • • • • • •

As you complete this chapter, reflect on what you've read, and record any additional thoughts or observations.

_____
_____
_____
_____
_____
_____
_____
_____
_____
_____
_____
_____
_____
_____
_____
_____
_____

12   Medical Health Insurance
        for Eating Disorders

Chapter 12 is all about insurance. We have listed four websites with insurance information and offered suggestions on how to navigate this ever-changing topic.

   After the introduction to this chapter, begin reading "Next Steps to Take Now." The topics are educational and complex, so take lots of notes.

Use this space to make a list of the websites you study and record your findings about insurance. Resources we suggest researching include:

- National Eating Disorders Association
- Center for Discovery
- Eating Disorder Hope
- Eating Recovery Center

_____

_____

_____

_____

_____

_____

_____

_____

_____

_____

_____

_____

_____

_____

_____

_____

_____

_____

_____

_____

• • • • • • • • • •

Review your insurance policy, and record your findings in the space below. Contact your insurance provider to understand what they need from you and to educate them with the knowledge you have acquired. When you speak with your insurance provider, take notes.

_____

_____

_____

_____

_____

_____

_____

_____

Get a confirmed diagnosis. What is it?

_____

_____

_____

Get preauthorization for treatment for your loved one. Call your insurance provider, and discuss this with them. Take notes in the space below.

_____

_____

_____

_____

_____

_____

_____

_____

_____

_____

Get confirmed billing codes. You can obtain these by calling the offices of the practitioners and professionals who are treating your loved one. Use the space below to write down those codes, then call your insurance company to make sure they recognize them.

_____   _____

_____   _____

_____   _____

_____   _____

Discuss coverage with human resources at your place of employment. Take notes in the space below.

_____

_____

_____

_____

_____

_____

_____

_____

_____

_____

Coverage for eating disorders and other mental illnesses is very complex. Please take thorough notes and prepare to be patient but assertive. Ask for help from anyone who understands the system better. Who might such an individual be?

_____

_____

_____

_____

_____

_____

_____

_____

_____

_____

_____

• • • • • • • • • •

As you complete this chapter, reflect on what you've read, and record any additional thoughts or observations.

_____

_____

_____

_____

_____

13

Other Ways and Means to Afford Treatment

Chapter 13 of *By Their Side* suggests many ways to help you afford treatment for your loved one. We discuss a variety of resources, online help, and free services.

Review the introduction to this chapter, then follow the suggestions in "Next Steps to Take Now." Take notes on the information applicable to your current situation.

_____

_____

_____

_____

_____

_____

_____

_____

_____

_____

_____

_____

_____

_____

_____

_____

_____

_____

This chapter lists websites we suggest reaching out to in order to find free consultations by phone with eating-disorder specialists. If you choose to reach out to any of them, use this space to keep track of your notes. As always, please do your own research if necessary.

- Eating Recovery Center
- Positive Pathways
- Eating Disorder Helpline Denver
- The Center: A Place of Hope
- Eating Disorder Recovery
- TreatingEatingDisorders.com
- Center for Discovery

_____

_____

_____

_____

_____

_____

_____

_____

_____

_____

_____

_____

_____

_____

_____

If you want to go a step further, contact the Elisa Project, and inquire about free case management. See *By Their Side* for more information.

• • • • • • • • • •

Do you enjoy reading blogs? Check out the list of blogs in this chapter of *By Their Side*, and read those that feel applicable to your situation. What did you learn? Journal and take notes in the space below.

_____

_____

_____

_____

_____

_____

_____

_____

_____

_____

_____

_____

_____

_____

Then review this chapter's suggestions of people who might be able to help you, and make a list of options from your community.

_____   _____

_____   _____

_____   _____

_____   _____

_____   _____

_____   _____

Research the variety of mentor programs, scholarships, resources, online parent forums, support groups, and online funding platforms suggested in this chapter, and make a list of those relevant to your situation.

_____

_____

_____

_____

_____

_____

_____

_____

_____

_____

· · · · · · · · · ·

Check out online therapy and therapy apps, and list those that might be applicable to your situation. In *By Their Side,* we suggest various articles to read on this topic, podcasts to listen to, and ten different eating-disorder apps to research. We do not endorse apps over personal, hands-on treatment, but some are potentially helpful. Please remember that most of these recommended apps are for caretakers, though a few are meant for the patient.

Are there specific apps you find helpful? List them here.

_____   _____

_____   _____

_____   _____

_____   _____

_____   _____

Is there an app for your loved one that seems suitable for their current situation? If so, consider sharing it with them. (Please note that before you choose to engage with any of the apps suggested in this chapter, we recommend checking with the doctors and professionals you are currently working with.)

• • • • • • • • • •

As you complete this chapter, reflect on what you've read, and record any additional thoughts or observations.

_____
_____
_____
_____
_____
_____
_____
_____
_____
_____
_____
_____
_____
_____
_____
_____
_____
_____
_____

14

Therapies, Practices, and Innovative Treatments

Chapter 14 of *By Their Side* provides resources on therapies, practices, and innovative treatments for eating disorders. We define different types of therapies, provide options, and suggest sites with further details.

Refer to this chapter's "Next Steps to Take Now" for suggested therapies, and make notes on ones that interest you. Some will be applicable to you or your loved one at this time, and others won't. For more information, please refer to the back of appendix of *By Their Side*.

> Please note that before you choose to engage in any of the treatments or therapies suggested in this chapter, we suggest you check with the doctors and professionals you are currently working with.

Take notes as you explore the therapies discussed in this chapter. They include:

- Naturopathic medicine
- Integrative medicine
- Integrative psychiatry
- Traditional Chinese medicine/ acupuncture
- Yoga
- Eye movement desensitization and reprocessing
- Extended care and aftercare treatment
- Solution-focused brief therapy
- Logotherapy
- Zero balancing
- Understanding emotional intelligence

- Hypnosis
- Equine therapy
- Pet therapy
- Referenced EEG
- Targeted nutritional therapy
- Online therapy and therapy apps
- Repetitive transcranial magnetic stimulation
- Deep brain stimulation
- Faith practices, meditation, and spiritual healing

_____
_____
_____
_____
_____
_____
_____
_____
_____
_____
_____
_____

• • • • • • • • • •

As you complete this chapter, reflect on what you've read, and record any additional thoughts or observations.

_____
_____
_____
_____
_____
_____
_____
_____
_____
_____
_____
_____

15

Service to Others

Chapter 15 of *By Their Side* is about service to others. In this chapter, we discuss timing, how to find the right fit, why service to others is beneficial to healing, and how to include your loved one and your family in your service work.

When the time is right, volunteer work can help in the recovery of eating disorders. If you decide to research volunteer opportunities in your community, use this space to keep track of and record your findings.

If the current timing is too sensitive for your loved one, consider other options that are not as intense or demanding. For instance, they might consider sponsoring a child internationally through monetary donations and letter writing; write advocacy letters on behalf of one of their passions; write letters to veterans or soldiers (if you are a military family, this might be ideal); blog; or respond to positive or uplifting social media accounts or sites.

Make a list of other service or volunteer ideas you are passionate about that would not require travel or additional stress. Can you include your loved one? Would this be a good topic of conversation to have with your loved one? Consider discussing why service to others is important, and see *By Their Side* for more ideas.

_____   _____

_____   _____

_____   _____

_____   _____

_____   _____

_____   _____

· · · · · · · · · ·

If your loved one is ready to volunteer and you want to share this experience with them, create a list of places at which you are interested in volunteering. Perhaps your place of worship? Local schools? The SPCA? A local soup kitchen? The library? Be creative, and find a good fit. There are many great websites that can help you begin this journey. List your findings here.

_____   _____

_____   _____

_____   _____

_____   _____

_____   _____

If you decide you want to volunteer alone, create your own list of possibilities.

_____   _____

_____   _____

_____   _____

_____   _____

_____   _____

Engaging in volunteer work or service to others is a personal decision, so you might need to reach out for help and educate yourself about what you can do. Call family members, friends, and acquaintances who work in the nonprofit sector, and ask for suggestions. Talk to anyone you know who has personal experience with a consistent volunteer job.

• • • • • • • • • •

As you complete this chapter, reflect on what you've read, and record any additional thoughts or observations.

_____

_____

_____

_____

16 Faith Practices

In chapter 16 of *By Their Side*, we look at how faith practices help you seek a higher power outside of yourself, how a lack of worthiness can heal, and how life is experienced not just in the tangible world but in the spiritual realm as well.

This is a deeply personal subject, so rather than suggesting next steps in this chapter, we offer words from our own personal experiences and quotations from professionals of different religions. Though they seemingly differ in their manner of devotion, praise, and glorification, faiths are actually very similar. They create community, proving time and again a natural human desire for something greater.

Do you have a desire for a close community? What would that look like?

_____

_____

_____

_____

_____

_____

Do you ever desire more? Do you find yourself constantly searching to better yourself physically, mentally, and spiritually, yet still needing more?

Do you have a faith practice? What does that look like for you?

_____

_____

_____

_____

_____

_____

_____

What are you looking for in your spiritual life? Is there anything that you want to be different?

_____

_____

_____

_____

_____

_____

How will you nurture your own personal faith? Do you pray or meditate? Do you have a place of worship? Do you reserve quiet time just for yourself and your faith practice? Do you have a daily routine to help calm your worries and feel peace in your soul? Journal in the space below as you reflect on what you desire.

_____

_____

_____

_____

_____

_____

_____

_____

_____

_____

_____

Do you not practice a faith? Are you interested in pursuing a spiritual life? If so, how would you begin that journey?

_____

_____

_____

_____

_____

_____

Are there days when you feel overwhelmed and don't know where to turn? To whom or what do you turn for comfort?

_____

_____

_____

_____

_____

_____

Our loved ones who are struggling with eating disorders can often feel a lack of significance and worthiness. In order to recover, one must have a sense of purpose and a broader perspective. Even in your pivotal role as a caretaker, you cannot fulfill the spiritual connection your loved one desires, but you can set an example.

Do you see yourself as a spiritual example for your loved one?

_____

_____

_____

_____

Can molding a faith practice help you with that? What would that look like for you?

_____

_____

_____

_____

_____

_____

> No matter whether your practice is labeled a religion or a way of life, the spiritual element of recovery plays a critical role in healing. We see this constantly in twelve-step recovery programs and faith-based healing.

Are you familiar with the philosophy of twelve-step recovery programs? If not, consider reading about them.

Please find a quiet place to reflect on and contemplate your faith. Each person's faith will look different, yet the yearning for peace and the belief that there is more to life than the physical is a common thread throughout all humanity. We sincerely hope that you can find that place of love and hope for yourself. Your example will not go unnoticed, and facing the demands of caretaking just might become more bearable.

> "In Hebrew, the word for *heaven* is *shamayim*. The word for *earth* is *aretz*. When you hear a Hebrew word that ends with *im*, it's a sign that word is plural. So what does this tell you?"
>
> "The word for heaven is plural . . . but the word for earth is not?"
>
> "Correct. *Shamayim*, heaven, is plural, but *aretz*, earth, is not. And it's not just the words; it's what the words represent."
>
> "Which is . . ."
>
> "That which is earthly is singular. That which belongs to the physical realm is finite. Everything that is physical is limited. That's why, no matter how much of the earthly realm you get, no matter how many earthly possessions you possess, it can never fill you or bring you completion."

"Because they're limited," I said, "because they're finite."

"And so a life focused on the physical . . ."

"Is a life filled with limitations."

"But if you empty your heart of physical things . . ."

"Then you empty yourself of limitations."

"So the things of earth are finite," he said, "but the things of heaven are infinite. The physical is limited, but the spiritual is unlimited. Only that which is spiritual, the infinite, can fill the heart."

"But how does one get away from living in the earthly realm?"

"One doesn't," said the teacher. "You can't escape living *in* the earthly realm—but you don't have to live *of* the earthly realm. You must deal with earthly things, but you don't have to fill your heart with them. Set your heart on that which is heavenly. Fill up your heart with that which is spiritual. For heaven is shamayim, and shamayim has no limitation. And, therefore, a heart filled up with that which is spiritual and that which is heavenly . . ."

"Becomes unlimited."[1]

• • • • • • • • • •

As you complete this chapter, please reflect on and record any additional thoughts or observations it may have prompted for you.

_____

_____

_____

_____

_____

_____

_____

_____

_____

_____

_____

_____

1   Jonathan Cahn, *The Book of Mysteries* (Lake Mary, Florida: FrontLine, 2016).

12 Closing

There really is no true closing to this book. The story is yours to continue. Your journey of healing is unique to you, your loved one, your friends, and your family. As you leave this book, consider the following questions.

What other aspects of healing might you and your family still need to explore?

_____

_____

_____

_____

_____

_____

_____

_____

_____

Have you learned anything new about yourself?

_____

_____

_____

_____

_____

_____

_____

_____

_____

_____

_____

_____

_____

Have you discovered anything about your family or loved ones that you were not familiar with?

_____

_____

_____

_____

_____

_____

_____

_____

_____

_____

_____

_____

Do you still have lots of questions? Please write them here.

_____

_____

_____

_____

_____

_____

_____

_____

_____

_____

_____

_____

_____

_____

_____

_____

Everything that you have written in this companion piece will afford you a deeper understanding of yourself, of others, of eating disorders, and of healing. Trust that this labor of learning and self-awareness will be the gift of a lifetime to you, your family, and your loved one. If there were any questions that you were unable to answer or sections in which you want to delve deeper, please consider going back and giving them another try. The time and effort are well worth it!

Please take this book and your answers to your therapist or counselor, and share your responses with those you trust.

Thank you for taking the time to read *By Their Side* and complete this workbook. We wish you and your loved one peace, blessings, and healing. Accept that you will still make mistakes. Give yourself grace, and aim for progress rather than perfection. We are rooting for you, and we believe in you. True recovery is possible, and freedom for you and your loved one is calling.

About the Author

Lara Lyn Bell represents the collective voice of this book's contributors, who have watched with fear, worry, and hope as their loved ones battled eating disorders. Bell is also comprised of trained professionals with experience in treating eating disorders. From medical doctors to therapists and psychologists, their extensive knowledge rounds out this supportive guide through the darkness of an ED to the light of whole healing. This book's contributors have combined forces because they have found that together is stronger than alone, and they want to offer that strength to anyone else who is fighting this battle.